Marty's Shape Adventure

a Hutterite shape book

written by
Elma Maendel

illustrated by
Cynthia Stahl

Text © 2008 Elma Maendel
Illustrations © 2008 Cynthia Stahl

Published in Canada by the

Box 40 MacGregor, Manitoba
R0H 0H0 CANADA
Phone: 1-204-272-5132
E-mail: orders@hbbookcentre.com
Web: www.hbbookcentre.com

All rights reserved.
Reproduction in whole or in part in any form or medium without express written permission is prohibited.

The publisher gratefully acknowledges Donna Gamache and Dora Maendel for their contributions.

First Edition - April 2007
Second Edition - June 2008
Third Edition - August 2023

Library and Archives Canada Cataloguing in Publication

Maendel, Elma, 1963-
Marty's adventure : a Hutterite shape book / Elma Maendel ; with illustrations by Cynthia Stahl.

ISBN 978-0-9780112-2-2

1. Shapes--Juvenile poetry. 2. Hutterian Brethren--Canada--Juvenile poetry. 3. Children's poetry, Canadian (English) I. Stahl, Cynthia, 1976- II. Title.

PS8626.A364M37 2008   jC811'.6   C2008-901278-X

for my students

When everyone is sleeping
I creep 'round Lizzie's house
To look for crumbs and cookies,
'Cause I'm clever Marty Mouse!

One night, as I am searching,
For yummy things to munch,
I notice something different
And forget about my lunch.

I spy shapes of many sizes,
And many colours too.
I find them all around me,
I'm certain, so can you!

Shhh! Lizzie's sleeping soundly
On her small rectangle bed.
Can you spy other rectangles
That are purple, blue or red?

An **oval** *Blachela* is on the floor
Where Lizzie's slippers lie.
Do you see any ovals
Why don't you have a try?

Blachela - Rug

A **triangle** *Tiechel* is fun to wear
For every Hutterite girl.
Do you see more triangles
As round the room you whirl?

Tiechel - kerchief

Lizzie has a tea party
With dishes neatly set.
Do you see any **circles**
On your *Puppela* or your pet?

Puppela – dolly

She keeps her **diamond** kite
Hanging on her *Schlofheisl* wall.
Can you see other diamonds
In the closet, room or hall?

Lizzie has a checker game
With **squares** of red and black.
Can you find any more squares
At the front, or at the back?

Schlofheisl – Bedroom

Now you can see that many shapes
Are here and also there.
Just take the time to look around,
You'll find them everywhere!

Elma Maendel

Elma Maendel teaches the primary grades at Brennan School on the Elm River Hutterite Community north of Newton, Manitoba, where she has lived all her life. For the past eight years she has been teacher/principal at Brennan. As a teen Elma had several stories and poems published in the *Western Producer*, but this is her first children's book.

Cynthia Stahl

Cynthia Kleinsasser Stahl has lived at Odanah Hutterite Community since 2001 when she married Harry Stahl. They have three children, Renae, Stefan and Darion. Cynthia has worked with children as a German teacher, but recently she was also elected to be *Essnschuel Ankela*, children's dining room supervisor. Cynthia has enjoyed art all her life and particularly enjoys drawing children and animals, using coloured pencil as her main medium.